JUDGE NOT!

7 Keys God Revealed
To Know How To Judge
And When To "Judge Not"

By Randy Clark

JUDGE NOT!
7 Keys God Revealed To Know How To Judge And When To "Judge Not"

©2016 RANDY CLARK
ISBN: 978-1-7324247-2-2

All rights reserved. No part of this book may be reproduced in any form or by any electronic or mechanical means, including information storage and retrieval systems, without written permission from the author, except in the case of a reviewer, who may quote brief passages embodied in critical articles or in a review.

Unless otherwise noted, all Scripture quotations are taken from the Holy Bible, New Living Translation, Copyright ©1996. Used by permission of Tyndale House Publishers, Inc., Wheaton, Illinois 60189. All rights reserved.

Scripture quotations marked (NKJV) are taken from the New King James Version® of the Bible. Copyright ©1982 by Thomas Nelson Inc.: Nashville. Used by permission. All rights reserved.

Underlining in Scripture quotations indicates the author's emphasis.

For more information about the author, go to:

www.RandyClark.info

Contents

Chapter 1: The Whole Truth 1

Chapter 2: Judging Truth 7

Chapter 3: Judging Conduct............................ 17

Chapter 4: Judging Yourself 27

Chapter 5: Judging Believers........................... 37

Chapter 6: Judging Unbelievers...................... 49

Chapter 7: The Judgment Seat 59

Chapter 8: Final Judgment............................... 71

Chapter 9: Final Thoughts 81

About the Author 93

Chapter 1
The Whole Truth

In America, before people can testify in court, they have to take an oath concerning the testimony they are about to give. Part of the oath is the statement that the person will "tell the truth, the whole truth and nothing but the truth." It is important to the judge and the jury to make sure they get the whole story and not just part of it. Sometimes a witness may want to leave out things that could help determine a person's guilt or innocence. Or they may want to mix a little truth and a little exaggeration. The jury is tasked with making a decision based on the facts of the case as presented in court. If they get a mixture of fact and fantasy, their decision will be tainted. Or if they only get a portion of the story, their decision will be flawed.

The same thing is true when you desire to know what God says in the Bible about a subject. The best way to get a full understanding of His revelation is to find out everything He said about the subject. That way you will be getting the "whole truth," and not just part of the truth. If you find one scripture you really like, but don't consider other teaching on the subject, you will have a distorted view of the truth. That one scripture may seem to support your preferred position, but maybe reading more on the subject will give you a better, more balanced assessment.

For example, did you know that the following statements are all found in the Bible?

"Judge not, that you be not judged."

"Do not judge according to appearance, but judge with righteous judgment."

"Take no part in the worthless deeds of evil and darkness; instead, expose them."

Chapter 1: The Whole Truth

"So don't make judgments about anyone ahead of time—before the Lord returns."

"But if we would examine ourselves, we would not be judged by God in this way."

"It isn't my responsibility to judge outsiders, but it certainly is your responsibility to judge those inside the church who are sinning."

"So what right do you have to judge your neighbor?"

"I say this because some ungodly people have wormed their way into your churches, saying that God's marvelous grace allows us to live immoral lives."

Some statements talk about "not judging" and some talk about how we <u>should</u> judge. So how do you reconcile all those verses in the Bible? They are all part of God's revelation to us. Yet, some of them seem to contradict each other. That is why it is so important to look for "the truth, the whole truth and nothing but the truth."

Paul was a man who lived in the early days of Christianity. He became a Christian and committed his life to Jesus after viciously opposing Him for a significant period of his life. He became a great leader in the church and, with the help of the Holy Spirit, wrote over half of what we call the New Testament portion of the Bible. On one of Paul's missionary journeys he asked for the church leaders in Ephesus to meet with him. The Holy Spirit had revealed to Paul that he would be arrested soon and face much adversity for living and proclaiming his Christian faith. Paul wanted to say goodbye to these faithful leaders because he knew he would not get a chance to come back that way again.

When they arrived he declared, "You know that from the day I set foot in the province of Asia until now I have done the Lord's work humbly and with many tears. I have endured the trials that came to me from the

Chapter 1: The Whole Truth

plots of the Jews. <u>I never shrank back from telling you what you needed to hear</u>, either publicly or in your homes. (Acts 20:18–20)

Paul wasn't afraid to tell them everything they needed to hear to live a life pleasing to God. He refused to back down from preaching the truth. Paul said he never held back any of the truth, regardless of the opposition that came his way.

"And indeed, now I know that you all, among whom I have gone preaching the kingdom of God, will see my face no more. Therefore I testify to you this day that I am innocent of the blood of all men. For I have not shunned to declare to you <u>the whole counsel of God</u>. (Acts 20:25–27)(NKJV)

Paul spent his later life preaching the "whole counsel of God"—the whole truth. As a result, he could say he was innocent of guilt if anyone chose to ignore his message. He gave them the truth, and it was their responsibility to believe it and act on it.

My goal in the rest of this book is to present to you the "whole counsel of God" concerning the subject of judging. It isn't as simple as some people present it. It has a variety of applications and nuances. So let's look at it from all different angles. Then you can make up your own mind after hearing "the truth, the whole truth and nothing but the truth" from God's revelation of truth to the world, the Bible.

Chapter 2
Judging Truth

SOMEBODY HAS TO SET THE STANDARD. Somebody had to decide the speed limit on a certain highway would be 60 mph. If you are stopped by a highway patrolman, you can't get out of a ticket by saying, "But I decided the speed limit should be 85 mph." Somebody had to decide that the work schedule for your job is from 7:00 a.m. to 3:30 p.m. You can't come to work at 10:00 a.m. and tell your boss, "But I decided my work schedule should start at 10:00 a.m." Somebody had to decide that the refrigerator you are purchasing will cost you $2,000. You can't give the appliance store $500 and tell them, "But I decided that $500 would work better for me than $2,000." These are all examples of the kind of issues we deal with in the natural world in which we live. We have to submit to other people's authority to make decisions in many areas of life.

But what about the spiritual and moral world? Who makes the decisions in that realm? Do we have to submit to anyone in that realm? Or can we each make our own decisions about truth and morality?

In today's world, many people would say that each person should be free to make their own decisions about morality. The pressure to be "politically correct" is so strong that many people submit to the idea that nobody should take a stand on anything because we may "offend" somebody. Many people take this concept so far that they would say "right and wrong" are defined by each person. Some would say that "truth" and "morality" are relative and not based on any absolute standard. Taking that thought to an extreme would mean that each person is capable of deciding for himself what is right and wrong.

I want to share something with you. The idea that each person can decide what is right and wrong is not a new thought. Do you know that is a concept that was presented to the first two human beings ever created by God? And it was not a concept presented by God. It was presented by the ultimate enemy of God.

Let me give you a little background on the story. God created a vast array of angelic beings to serve Him. The angel in charge of the whole bunch was named Lucifer. He was a beautiful creature, capable of creating music and worship to his Creator God. But Lucifer wasn't content with being number two in the universe. He wanted God's throne. He hatched a scheme and convinced a third of the angels to join him in a rebellion against God. His plan didn't work. Nobody can defeat Almighty God. Lucifer - the dragon—the serpent—the devil—Satan; however he is described, he lost the battle. Here is how the event is described in the Bible.

Then there was war in heaven. Michael and his angels fought against the dragon and his angels. And the dragon lost the battle, and he and his angels were forced out of

heaven. This great dragon—the ancient serpent called the devil, or <u>Satan, the one deceiving the whole world</u>—was thrown down to the earth with all his angels. (Revelation 12:7–9)

Satan, the deceiver, spent a long time pondering his mistake after he was cast out of heaven. He is a spirit being and was present when God created the first humans called Adam and Eve. God put Adam and Eve in a beautiful garden on earth and gave them only one restriction.

The Lord God placed the man in the Garden of Eden to tend and watch over it. But the Lord God warned him, "You may freely eat the fruit of every tree in the garden — except the tree of the knowledge of good and evil. If you eat its fruit, you are sure to die." (Genesis 2:15–17)

Satan wanted to usurp God's place of ultimate authority and power. His direct rebellion

CHAPTER 2: JUDGING TRUTH

against God didn't work, so he approached God's new creation with a temptation to try to separate them from God. He brought a new thought to Eve. It is the same thought "politically correct" folks are thinking today.

The serpent was the shrewdest of all the wild animals the Lord God had made. One day he asked the woman, "Did God really say you must not eat the fruit from any of the trees in the garden?" "Of course we may eat fruit from the trees in the garden," the woman replied. It's only the fruit from the tree in the middle of the garden that we are not allowed to eat. God said, 'You must not eat it or even touch it; if you do, you will die.' " "You won't die!" the serpent replied to the woman. "God knows that your eyes will be opened as soon as you eat it, and <u>you will be like God, knowing both good and evil</u>." (Genesis 3:1–5)

Satan told Eve that eating the forbidden fruit would enable her to "be like God." Satan fed her the lie that she would then be able to "know" both good and evil. Satan deceived Eve with the lie that she could be like God and decide for herself what was good and what was evil. That can be an intoxicating thought! You can be "like God!" Isn't that what many people in today's world are saying? Aren't they saying that each person can decide if something is right or wrong or good or evil or moral or immoral? Isn't that the thought motivating those who would shout, "Judge not!" whenever anyone dares to question their conduct? After all, if you are "like God," and can decide for yourself what is right and wrong, than nobody else can judge your actions, can they?

The Source of Truth

God is the source of all truth. Since He created mankind, He has ultimate authority over His creation. God, the Father; Jesus, the Son; and the Holy Spirit, make up what some people refer to as "The Trinity." They are all God and

CHAPTER 2: JUDGING TRUTH

they all agree. God has provided us with a record of His truth. We call that record, the Bible.

"My thoughts are nothing like your thoughts," says the Lord. "And my ways are far beyond anything you could imagine. For just as the heavens are higher than the earth, so my ways are higher than your ways and my thoughts higher than your thoughts. "The rain and snow come down from the heavens and stay on the ground to water the earth. They cause the grain to grow, producing seed for the farmer and bread for the hungry. It is the same with my word. I send it out, and it always produces fruit. It will accomplish all I want it to, and it will prosper everywhere I send it. (Isaiah 55:8–11)

God said that He sent His heavenly thoughts down to the earth just like the rain and snow come from the heavens down to the earth. He sent His word to help us learn how to live a life of joy by obeying His truth. Look at portions of a prayer Jesus prayed to His Father as He neared the end of His time on earth.

"Now I am coming to you. I told them many things while I was with them in this world so they would be filled with my joy. (John 17:13)

Jesus told us that there would be those in this world who would hate us and oppose us if we choose to put God's words of truth above man's opinions.

I have given them your word. And the world hates them because they do not belong to the world, just as I do not belong to the world. (John 17:14)

Jesus made it clear that, although we live in a corrupt world, we don't really belong here. Our citizenship is in heaven. But a Christian's ultimate destination is heaven only because of the grace of God and the fact that Jesus paid the penalty for sin for us. We are all sinners who need forgiveness. Christians just look to a higher power for the wisdom and strength to obey the truths found in the Bible.

I'm not asking you to take them out of the world, but to keep them safe from the evil one. They do not belong to this world any more than I do. (John 17:15–16)

Jesus made it clear that He spoke the truth as He continued to pray to His Father.

Make them holy by your truth; teach them your word, which is truth. (John 17:17)

Jesus always spoke the truth. Regardless of what anyone says, we will ultimately be judged on God's word and not on what we decided we should be judged on. God is the ultimate authority to whom we must submit.

But all who reject me and my message will be judged on the day of judgment by the truth I have spoken. (John 12:48)

Because of what we have looked at in this chapter, the rest of this book is based on what God has revealed to us in His word about when to judge, how to judge and when not to judge.

Chapter 3
Judging Conduct

We all judge people's conduct nearly every day. You decide if you like the waiter's service at a restaurant. You judge your dentist's ability and conduct. You judge someone to determine if he/she is someone you would want to date or maybe marry. You judge when you decide who you want as a friend.

In America, we have judges who make decisions on people's conduct. Stealing from another person is judged unacceptable and is considered illegal conduct. Lying while giving testimony in a court case is judged as perjury and is not tolerated. If you read a newspaper article that describes a person as being found guilty of murder, surely you agree that murdering conduct is wrong.

And yet, many people will attack a person for speaking the truth. In today's world, some folks seem to look for a reason to be "offended" whenever anyone makes a statement contrary to their personal belief. Unfortunately, many of the offended folks take it a step further and accuse someone of "hating" if they dare speak a word against conduct they deem acceptable.

A person who speaks out and says that stealing and murder are wrong should not be considered a person who hates thieves and murderers. A person who speaks out against cheating on your spouse should not be considered a person who hates all cheaters. <u>Speaking the truth about immoral conduct isn't the same as judging a person's heart or eternal destiny</u>. Judging conduct as good or bad is something we all do regularly.

Proclaim Tolerance or the Truth?

Jesus took some strong positions while He was on this earth. Everybody didn't agree with

CHAPTER 3: JUDGING CONDUCT

everything He said. In fact, some people got so mad at Him that they wanted to kill Him! Even His Jewish brothers, who were all descendants of Abraham, couldn't handle the truth.

Yes, I realize that you are descendants of Abraham. And yet some of you are trying to kill me because there's no room in your hearts for my message. (John 8:37)

After that, he taught daily in the Temple, but the leading priests, the teachers of religious law, and the other leaders of the people began planning how to kill him. But they could think of nothing, because all the people hung on every word he said. (Luke 19:47–48)

The religious folks thought they already had all the answers. And when Jesus taught them the truth, they rebelled and looked for a way to silence Him forever. Some people don't like to hear the truth. But Jesus said we all need to hear the truth. And the truth is found in the Bible, God's word to mankind. Look at a portion of a prayer Jesus prayed for all who will believe His message.

They do not belong to this world any more than I do. Make them holy by your truth; <u>teach them your word, which is truth</u>. Just as you sent me into the world, I am sending them into the world. And I give myself as a holy sacrifice for them so <u>they can be made holy by your truth</u>. (John 17:16–19)

Somebody has to proclaim the truth of God's word. People can't choose to obey and live as God wants them to unless they know the truth. Proclaiming the truth forces a person to make a decision. We all have to choose to obey God or ignore Him. Over our lifetimes, we all fall short many times and need God's forgiveness for our weaknesses and failures. But as long as we know the truth, we know whether we are rejecting God or submitting to Him with our obedience.

Jesus was very "intolerant" of those who disagreed with Him. He came across as intolerant because truth is truth. For example,

Jesus told people He was the only way to be saved and that nobody could reach God except through Him. That sounds very narrow-minded, doesn't it? But it is the truth.

Jesus told him, "I am the way, the truth, and the life. No one can come to the Father except through me. (John 14:6)

Jesus preached that we should love each other, but He never preached that all behavior should be "tolerated." In one instance, Jesus confronted a woman who had been caught in the act of having sex with a man who was not her husband. Jesus demonstrated His love by offering her forgiveness. But then He made it clear her conduct was sinful and that she should not repeat her sinful behavior.

Then Jesus stood up again and said to the woman, "Where are your accusers? Didn't even one of them condemn you?" "No, Lord," she said. And Jesus said, "Neither do I. Go and sin no more." (John 8:10–11)

God knows that sinful behavior is harmful. God doesn't want people to be hurt by the results of sinful conduct during their lives on earth. And He certainly doesn't want anyone to spend eternity in hell because of unforgiven sin. His word is like a light that illuminates the path and helps us avoid obstacles that can harm us. *"Your word is a lamp to guide my feet and a light for my path." (Psalm 119:105)* Sin must be exposed by the light of God's word so we can avoid it and avoid the consequences it brings.

Therefore, proclaiming the truth is actually an act of love and not hate. The truth can serve as a warning of danger ahead if a person continues to ignore the light of God's word. When a person proclaims the truth of God's word, that truth should be welcomed and not resisted because it will help a person live a fruitful, successful life.

Don't be fooled by those who try to excuse these sins, for the anger of God will fall on all who disobey him. Don't participate in the things these people do. For once you were *full of darkness, but now you have light from the Lord. So live as people of light! For this light within you produces only what is good and right and true. Carefully determine what pleases the Lord. <u>Take no part in the worthless deeds of evil and darkness; instead, expose them</u>. (Ephesians 5:6–11)*

Some people in today's world have taken the position that since God is love that means we can do anything we want with no consequences. Some even have an extreme belief that God's grace has already forgiven us for any sin we will ever commit so we can live as we wish without any consequences. They reject any attempt to control their behavior. That is an old argument that was circulating even during the early days of the church. It is a false argument meant to deceive people and keep them enslaved to sin. The grace of God is a wonderful thing. God's forgiveness for sin is certainly available to a Christian. But God's grace should not be abused by ignoring God's instructions and continuing to blatantly sin.

Dear friends, I had been eagerly planning to write to you about the salvation we all share. But now I find that I must write about something else, urging you to defend the faith that God has entrusted once for all time to his holy people. I say this because <u>some ungodly people have wormed their way into your churches, saying that God's marvelous grace allows us to live immoral lives</u>. The condemnation of such people was recorded long ago, for they have denied our only Master and Lord, Jesus Christ. (Jude 3–4)

Persecution

If you proclaim the truth you will make some people mad. And sometimes angry people will strike out and accuse you of being a "hater." Paul dealt with the same thing in the early days of the church. He realized that pleasing God should be more important than pleasing people.

Chapter 3: Judging Conduct

Obviously, I'm not trying to win the approval of people, but of God. If pleasing people were my goal, I would not be Christ's servant. (Galatians 1:10)

Persecution for proclaiming the truth and judging conduct has been around a long time. Remember, I am not talking about judging someone's character or motives. I am not talking about condemning people and telling them they are going to hell. I am simply referring to stating that some actions and lifestyles are wrong and harmful according to God's word. Remember that you are not making a judgment about sin. You are simply agreeing with God and delivering His truth about sin. And there is one good thing about being persecuted for proclaiming the truth. You will one day be rewarded for your difficulties!

"God blesses you when people mock you and persecute you and lie about you and say all sorts of evil things against you because you are my followers. Be happy about it! Be

very glad! For a great reward awaits you in heaven... (Matthew 5:11–12)

People can be hurtful. People can question your motives. People can react with great passion to justify their behavior. But we don't get to decide what is right and what is wrong. We can't negate God's word and say it doesn't apply anymore. None of us can re-write the Bible and say today's culture demands that God change His mind about conduct that is against His nature. His word is given to help us, not harm us. We have a choice to listen to what God is saying or ignore Him.

All Scripture is inspired by God and is useful to teach us what is true and to make us realize what is wrong in our lives. It corrects us when we are wrong and teaches us to do what is right. God uses it to prepare and equip his people to do every good work. (2 Timothy 3:16–17)

Chapter 4
Judging Yourself

God's grace is a wonderful blessing. Receiving His grace means God gives us something we don't deserve. Forgiveness is something we don't deserve. But God offers it freely to those who will repent of their sin and ask for His forgiveness. Forgiveness enables us to have an unbroken fellowship with God. That should be a goal of all Christians, to never allow anything to keep us from a free and open communication with our Heavenly Father.

That means we have to be aware of sinful actions we have committed which need to be forgiven. Self-examination is necessary to allow the Holy Spirit to show us areas of our lives which need correction and forgiveness. There are times we need to "judge ourselves" by asking the Holy Spirit to reveal actions and behaviors that are not pleasing to God.

One of the best times to conduct this self-examination is when we take communion, or observe the Lord's Supper. This is a time where we remember the sacrifice of Jesus by partaking, in a similar way, of the bread and juice that Jesus shared with His disciples the night he was betrayed. This should be a sacred and meaningful remembrance of everything Jesus accomplished for us through His death and resurrection. It should never be conducted with jokes or in an irreverent way.

In Bible days, the church members in the city of Corinth were not conducting themselves in a manner worthy of the worship of Jesus. Paul had to address their conduct in the first letter he sent to the Corinthians. Many of the church members were simply having a party, selfishly eating a big meal before their observance of the Lord's Supper. Others were insistent on maintaining their cliques of division instead of welcoming all believers equally.

Chapter 4: Judging Yourself

Some were even overindulging on wine to the point of drunkenness. Paul delivers a serious rebuke to this kind of behavior.

But in the following instructions, I cannot praise you. For it sounds as if more harm than good is done when you meet together. First, I hear that there are divisions among you when you meet as a church, and to some extent I believe it. But, of course, there must be divisions among you so that you who have God's approval will be recognized! When you meet together, you are not really interested in the Lord's Supper. For some of you hurry to eat your own meal without sharing with others. As a result, some go hungry while others get drunk. What? Don't you have your own homes for eating and drinking? Or do you really want to disgrace God's church and shame the poor? What am I supposed to say? Do you want me to praise you? Well, I certainly will not praise you for this! (1 Corinthians 11:17–22)

Jesus told His disciples to continue to conduct this rite as a way to remember that He gave His body and His blood to deliver us from the penalty for our sins. We all come to the cross the same way. We all need God's grace and mercy. We all approach God the same way and that is only through the blood of Jesus which makes us righteous. Jesus said to continue to partake of the wine (or grape juice) and bread as a way to remember His death on the cross to pay the ultimate price for our sins.

For I pass on to you what I received from the Lord himself. On the night when he was betrayed, the Lord Jesus took some bread and gave thanks to God for it. Then he broke it in pieces and said, "This is my body, which is given for you. Do this to remember me." In the same way, he took the cup of wine after supper, saying, "This cup is the new covenant between God and his people—an agreement confirmed with my blood. Do this to remember me as often as you drink it." For every time you eat this bread and drink this cup,

you are announcing the Lord's death until he comes again. (1 Corinthians 11:23–26)

This observance should never be taken lightly. This really happened the last night Jesus spent with His disciples before His death. The next day, Jesus' body would be horribly beaten. The flesh on His back would be ripped open as He was savagely whipped. His blood would flow when the Roman soldiers mocked Jesus by pressing a crown of thorns into his head. Blood flowed from His hands and feet as he was brutally nailed to a wooden cross. The physical pain Jesus experienced was excruciating. The blood that flowed from His injuries was the pure blood of God. It was powerful enough to provide salvation to anyone who would ever live and accept His sacrifice.

Observing communion means remembering the tremendous sacrifice Jesus provided as an act of His love. Because of the incredible price He paid for our sins, we should never treat sin lightly. We should look in our own heart and ask the Holy Spirit to illuminate sins for which we need cleansing. If any are brought to mind, we should judge that sin to be unacceptable, confess it and ask God for forgiveness. If we are harboring unforgiveness toward another, we should judge that unforgiveness to be unacceptable and forgive the person who has wronged us. This should all be done before we take the communion elements to commemorate the sacrifice Jesus gave for our sins.

If we are not taking advantage of God's forgiveness for our sins, then we are not properly discerning and honoring the purpose of Jesus giving His body and blood. If we are not releasing those who have harmed us by forgiving them, than we are not worthy of receiving God's forgiveness. Neglecting to forgive and be forgiven can cause a person to be physically sick and even die before that person's time.

So anyone who eats this bread or drinks this cup of the Lord unworthily is guilty of sinning against the body and blood of the Lord. That is why you should examine yourself

Chapter 4: Judging Yourself

before eating the bread and drinking the cup. For if you eat the bread or drink the cup without honoring the body of Christ, you are eating and drinking God's judgment upon yourself. That is why many of you are weak and sick and some have even died. (1 Corinthians 11:27–30)

Judging, or examining, ourselves, is better than allowing sins to continue to the point that God decides to step in and discipline us Himself. God's discipline is always for our own good. However, it is always better to stop undesirable behavior on our own and then ask for God's forgiveness. I would always rather receive God's grace due to my mistakes instead of His discipline.

But if we would examine ourselves, we would not be judged by God in this way. Yet when we are judged by the Lord, we are being disciplined so that we will not be condemned along with the world. (1 Corinthians 11:31–32)

Anytime—Anywhere

Judging ourselves before we take communion is a necessary discipline to develop. However, that is not the only time we can receive God's forgiveness. The Holy Spirit will stir your conscience as a believer to let you know you have sinned. That can happen anytime. At home. At work. In your car. In church. When you are somewhere you shouldn't be. The important thing is to respond quickly when the Holy Spirit convicts you of sin in your life. Judge yourself by admitting what you have done is a sin and follow this scriptural mandate:

If we claim we have no sin, we are only fooling ourselves and not living in the truth. But if we confess our sins to him, he is faithful and just to forgive us our sins and to cleanse us from all wickedness. (1 John 1:8–9)

An especially good time to judge yourself is before you ask God for something during a prayer time. Make sure you aren't holding a grudge in your heart toward someone who has hurt you. Holding a grudge is another way to say refusing to forgive. Forgiveness is really important to God. He gave His all to provide forgiveness for us and He expects us to extend the same to others. Even when they are in the wrong.

But when you are praying, first forgive anyone you are holding a grudge against, so that your Father in heaven will forgive your sins, too." (Mark 11:25)

Jesus included this admonition when He taught His disciples how to pray. Immediately following His instruction to ask for forgiveness, He includes the declaration that we should already have forgiven those who have sinned against us.

Pray like this: Our Father in heaven, may your name be kept holy. May your Kingdom come soon. May your will be done on earth, as it is in heaven. Give us today the food *we need, and <u>forgive us our sins, as we have forgiven those who sin against us</u>. And don't let us yield to temptation, but rescue us from the evil one. "If you forgive those who sin against you, your heavenly Father will forgive you. But if you refuse to forgive others, your Father will not forgive your sins. (Matthew 6:9–15)*

Judging ourselves is a necessary and critical part of life. Staying free from unconfessed sin will keep you in an unhindered fellowship and communion with God.

Chapter 5
Judging Believers

God is smarter than you and me. I hope you can accept that as truth. If I have to convince you of that reality, then you might as well stop reading this book. God created humans and he understands their weaknesses. He understands what life is all about since He is the creator of it all. There is a reason God wants us to stay away from sin. It is very simple. Sin is harmful. Sin will hinder your fellowship and communication with God. Sin will cloud your judgment. The fruit of sin is not good. Some sins can be fun for a while, but they will eventually create problems in the life of a sinner and others in his life.

If you love a family member, you wouldn't want that person to be harmed, would you? If your sister is distracted and about to walk barefooted into a fire ant nest, wouldn't you tell her to stop? Those who have trusted in Jesus are all part of the family of God. You should be able to talk to a family member about things you would not consider discussing with a stranger or even an acquaintance.

God decided in advance to adopt us into his own family by bringing us to himself through Jesus Christ. This is what he wanted to do, and it gave him great pleasure. (Ephesians 1:5)

So what should you do if you are a believer and you see another "family member" living a sinful lifestyle? Should we ignore it because we don't want to judge anyone? Or should we take a different view when it comes to our fellow believers? Remember, sin is harmful and you don't want to see anyone you love get hurt.

Chapter 5: Judging Believers

Your Attitude Matters

We are all sinners. We are all subject to temptation. When we approach a fellow believer about sin, we must remember that we are not "better" than the person struggling with sin. We are all in need of God's grace and forgiveness. If we are living our life free from a certain sin, it is by learning to depend on Jesus and His power to help us and not because of our own greatness. Jesus told a story about a man who was full of pride because he thought he was better than someone struggling with sin. Jesus told this story to a group of people who thought they were living on a higher spiritual plane and who looked down on others who were dealing with sin in their lives.

Then Jesus told this story to some who had great confidence in their own righteousness and scorned everyone else: "Two men went to the Temple to pray. One was a Pharisee, and the other was a despised tax collector.

JUDGE NOT!

The Pharisee stood by himself and prayed this prayer: 'I thank you, God, that I am not a sinner like everyone else. For I don't cheat, I don't sin, and I don't commit adultery. I'm certainly not like that tax collector! I fast twice a week, and I give you a tenth of my income.' "But the tax collector stood at a distance and dared not even lift his eyes to heaven as he prayed. Instead, he beat his chest in sorrow, saying, 'O God, be merciful to me, for I am a sinner.' I tell you, this sinner, not the Pharisee, returned home justified before God. For those who exalt themselves will be humbled, and those who humble themselves will be exalted." (Luke 18:9–14)

Notice that the person God helped was the one who cried out for His mercy. The one who was full of pride in his accomplishments was not justified in God's eyes. We can only be "righteous" or "justified" before God when we admit we are sinners and ask for God's forgiveness. Righteousness, which means right standing with God, is a gift that can only be received when we put out trust in Jesus. Righteousness is not something you can earn.

For the sin of this one man, Adam, caused death to rule over many. But even greater is God's wonderful grace and his <u>gift of righteousness</u>, for all who receive it will live in triumph over sin and death through this one man, Jesus Christ. (Romans 5:17)

So before you approach a fellow believer about sin in his life, make sure that you have a proper attitude. You can just as easily be caught up in the same sin if you aren't leaning on the mercy and grace of God. Your approach to your friend and fellow believer could start with the declaration that you are in need of God's grace and forgiveness every day.

Your Motivation Matters

Your motivation to confront a fellow believer should be to help them. You shouldn't want to embarrass a person when you talk to them about something in their life they need to change. That is why you would normally want to speak to someone privately about the matter and to keep your conversation private in the future. The motivation to point out sin in another believer's life is to avoid harm to the believer and restore them to a place of unhindered fellowship with God.

You should also set a goal not to get into an argument which could cause the person to be defensive about their decisions. Sin can open the door to the devil to cause serious problems in a person's life. Be gentle and kind when you speak with a friend about their problems.

Again I say, don't get involved in foolish, ignorant arguments that only start fights. A servant of the Lord must not quarrel but must be kind to everyone, be able to teach, and be patient with difficult people. <u>Gently instruct those who oppose the truth</u>. Perhaps God will change those people's hearts, and they will learn the truth. Then they *will come to their senses and escape from the devil's trap. For they have been held captive by him to do whatever he wants. (2 Timothy 2:23–26)*

Nobody is too important to help another believer in need. Just remember, your purpose in the whole matter is to help get the person out of trouble. Treat them the way you would want to be treated if you were caught up in sin that was causing problems in your life. Realize that you could easily be involved in the same type of sin. You don't want to enable someone by telling them their behavior is understandable. But you should offer to help them overcome their struggles. Offer to regularly pray with them, talk with them and hold them accountable to not repeat their actions. Be a friend just like you need a friend when you are facing difficulties in life.

Dear brothers and sisters, if <u>another believer</u> is overcome by some sin, you who are godly should gently and humbly help that *person back onto the right path. And be careful not to fall into the same temptation yourself. Share each other's burdens, and in this way obey the law of Christ. If you think you are too important to help someone, you are only fooling yourself. You are not that important. (Galatians 6:1–3)*

They most likely already know what they are doing is wrong in God's eyes. But they may not think it is serious enough to stop. Or they may not think they have the ability to change their behavior. Or maybe they just need someone like you to tell them you support them and will help them recover and get back on the right path.

Your Church Family Matters

In very rare occasions, a person's sin could have a negative effect on his local church body of believers. If a person is living in blatant sin, and is unwilling to repent and get help to change his conduct, sometimes a public rebuke is necessary. This is necessary to ensure that church members do not think that obvious, sinful behavior is something to ignore and condone. However, a public rebuke should always be a last resort, after numerous attempts to resolve the issue privately. It should never happen without consulting with your local church's pastor and leadership team. And it should certainly never happen without much prayer beforehand.

Those who sin should be reprimanded in front of the whole church; this will serve as a strong warning to others. (1 Timothy 5:20)

Publically addressing a church member's sin will have an effect throughout the church family. But in extremely rare circumstances, it may be necessary to make sure the church family realizes the seriousness of continued, blatant sin. The grace of God should never be misused to condone serious, public sin.

Dear friends, I had been eagerly planning to write to you about the salvation we all share. But now I find that I must write about something else, urging you to defend the faith that God has entrusted once for all time to his holy people. I say this because <u>some ungodly people have wormed their way into your churches, saying that God's marvelous grace allows us to live immoral lives</u>. The condemnation of such people was recorded long ago, for they have denied our only Master and Lord, Jesus Christ. (Jude 3–4)

A public rebuke may be delivered in a variety of ways and even in steps. It could be before only the pastoral team at first. If the behavior continues, a reprimand in front of the church elders, a group of friends, or, in extreme cases, before the entire local church family may be necessary. Once again, a public rebuke before the entire church is a last resort and should only be accomplished under the direction of your church pastor and leaders.

CHAPTER 5: JUDGING BELIEVERS

When I wrote to you before, I told you not to associate with people who indulge in sexual sin. But I wasn't talking about unbelievers who indulge in sexual sin, or are greedy, or cheat people, or worship idols. You would have to leave this world to avoid people like that. I meant that you are not to associate with anyone <u>who claims to be a believer</u> yet indulges in sexual sin, or is greedy, or worships idols, or is abusive, or is a drunkard, or cheats people. Don't even eat with such people. It isn't my responsibility to judge outsiders, but <u>it certainly is your responsibility to judge those inside the church who are sinning</u>. God will judge those on the outside; but as the Scriptures say, "You must remove the evil person from among you." (1 Corinthians 5:9–13)

Remember that the reason for confronting a believer who is living in serious sin is to help rescue them from the result of sin. Restoration and forgiveness is always the ultimate goal.

Chapter 6
Judging Unbelievers

EVERY PERSON ON EARTH CAN BE PLACED IN one of two categories. Those who are part of the Kingdom of God and those who are part of the kingdom of darkness. I know that sounds harsh, but the Bible is clear about it. If you have been born again, you are part of God's kingdom. If you have not put your trust in Jesus, you are in Satan's kingdom, ruled by the forces of darkness.

For he has rescued us from the kingdom of darkness and transferred us into the Kingdom of his dear Son, who purchased our freedom and forgave our sins. (Colossians 1:13–14)

We were all part of the kingdom of darkness at one time because of the inherent sin in each of us. The only way to get out is to trust in the magnificent sacrifice Jesus made for us. None of us can earn our way into the Kingdom of God. We can only get there because of the grace of God. Once a person is saved, it doesn't mean that person is superior to anyone else. It just means he has admitted he needs help and reached out to Jesus for a new beginning.

Jesus told us how to be transferred from Satan's kingdom to God's kingdom. He called it being "born again." The born again experience creates a change in a person's heart, or spirit. Only after the heart has been changed can a person truly have the desire to serve God and have the help of the Holy Spirit to do so. Look at how Jesus explained the difference between physical and spiritual birth to a leading religious leader.

There was a man of the Pharisees named Nicodemus, a ruler of the Jews. This man came to Jesus by night and said to Him,

CHAPTER 6: JUDGING UNBELIEVERS

"Rabbi, we know that You are a teacher come from God; for no one can do these signs that You do unless God is with him." Jesus answered and said to him, "Most assuredly, I say to you, <u>unless one is born again</u>, he cannot see the kingdom of God." Nicodemus said to Him, "How can a man be born when he is old? Can he enter a second time into his mother's womb and be born?" Jesus answered, "Most assuredly, I say to you, unless one is born of water and the Spirit, he cannot enter the kingdom of God. That which is born of the flesh is flesh, and that which is born of the Spirit is spirit. Do not marvel that I said to you, 'You must be born again.' The wind blows where it wishes, and you hear the sound of it, but cannot tell where it comes from and where it goes. So is everyone who is born of the Spirit." (John 3:1–8)

Once the human spirit, or heart, is changed, then God can begin to mold a person into the image of Jesus. Once you begin to truly worship God, make Him a priority and delight in

Him, He will give you desires that align with His will. And when you commit those new desires to Him, He will help you see those desires become reality.

Take delight in the Lord, and he will give you your heart's desires. Commit everything you do to the Lord. Trust him, and he will help you. (Psalm 37:4–5)

Once we are part of God's kingdom, the Holy Spirit will help us live the kind of life God desires for us. Even after we are transferred into the Kingdom of God, we will still falter and sin. But forgiveness is always available because of the grace of God.

If we claim we have no sin, we are only fooling ourselves and not living in the truth. But if we confess our sins to him, he is faithful and just to forgive us our sins and to cleanse us from all wickedness. (1 John 1:8–9)

Many people who are not Christians do not have the motivation to follow the teachings from the Bible. If a person is not born again, that person does not see Jesus as Lord or someone to obey. People may make good moral choices, but without making a commitment to serve Jesus, the desire to obey God is just not there in the same way it is for a Christian. Because when we are saved, God helps us by changing our desires to line up with His desires. He will help us want the same things that He wants.

For God is working in you, giving you the desire and the power to do what pleases him. (Philippians 2:13)

Don't Judge

Because of everything I just explained, people who have not yet made a commitment to serve Jesus should not be held to the same standards as a Christian. We should not be judging a person as if they were part of the Kingdom of God if they have not made that commitment.

Let me give you an example. I am an American citizen by birth. I am accountable to obey the laws of the United States of America. However, it would not be fair to hold me accountable to obey the laws of China, or Japan, or Australia or any other country because I am not a citizen of those countries.

In the same way, my allegiance is to God and His kingdom and my true spiritual citizenship is in heaven. I made a choice to be a part of that kingdom and pledge my allegiance to Jesus as my Lord. I did that when I was born again by putting my trust in Jesus for my salvation.

For our citizenship is in heaven, from which we also eagerly wait for the Savior, the Lord Jesus Christ (Philippians 3:20)

For those who have not yet made that decision, they can't be expected to obey the same commands that a Christian has committed to follow. Our responsibility to unbelievers is simply to love them. <u>A Christian should not judge unbelievers</u>. We don't need to point out any particular sin in their lives. We shouldn't look down on them. We shouldn't try to show them how holy and righteous we may think we are. We should be a light to help them understand the wonderful grace and mercy that is available through Jesus. We should love them and be willing to share the good news that changed our lives. Jesus is the focal point of the gospel message, not us or our conduct.

Jesus' Example

Jesus was criticized because He was willing to spend time with people that the religious leaders knew were unrepentant sinners. Jesus chose to show them love instead of judgment. He knew their lifestyles were sinful and He certainly didn't approve of their choices. But Jesus knew He wouldn't be able to impact their lives until He demonstrated His love first. Here is one example.

JUDGE NOT!

Jesus entered Jericho and made his way through the town. There was a man there named Zacchaeus. He was the chief tax collector in the region, and he had become very rich. He tried to get a look at Jesus, but he was too short to see over the crowd. So he ran ahead and climbed a sycamore-fig tree beside the road, for Jesus was going to pass that way. When Jesus came by, he looked up at Zacchaeus and called him by name. "Zacchaeus!" he said. "Quick, come down! I must be a guest in your home today." Zacchaeus quickly climbed down and took Jesus to his house in great excitement and joy. But the people were displeased. <u>"He has gone to be the guest of a notorious sinner,"</u> they grumbled. Meanwhile, Zacchaeus stood before the Lord and said, "I will give half my wealth to the poor, Lord, and if I have cheated people on their taxes, I will give them back four times as much!" Jesus responded, "Salvation has come to this home today, for this man has shown himself to be a true

son of Abraham. <u>For the Son of Man came to seek and save those who are lost</u>." (Luke 19:1–10)

If you want to impact an unbeliever's life in the best way possible, you should love them. If you love someone, you want what is best for them. What is best is that they would be born again so they will not suffer the eternal punishment for their sin. And what is best is that their heart would be changed so they will begin to desire to leave their sinful habits behind and pursue a new direction. The heart change has to come first. Then the behavior changes will follow.

Shortly before Jesus finished His physical life on earth, He told His disciples something powerful. He said people will know you belong to Him because you demonstrate the love of God towards others. Notice He did not say you would reveal God to people by your judgments of all the areas where unbelievers are sinning and falling short of God's perfection. He said you need to show people the love of

God. God sees people's potential and not just their failures.

So now I am giving you a new commandment: Love each other. Just as I have loved you, you should love each other. Your love for one another will prove to the world that you are my disciples." (John 13:34–35)

Unbelievers need to know you care about their eternity. Most people already know they are sinners. They need to know how to be saved. They need to know that you are a sinner, too. And that we all come to the cross of Jesus the same way. We all need God's matchless grace and mercy to remove the guilt and condemnation for our sins.

Chapter 7

The Judgment Seat

Most people like to be rewarded for their efforts. For your job, a reward may be a salary bonus, an increase in pay, a special gift or even just a public "thank you" from your boss. When we know a reward is coming, that keeps us motivated to consistently do the right thing.

Did you know that you can qualify for rewards from God? You can! For a Christian, Jesus has scheduled a special awards ceremony to give you exactly what you deserve for the life you have lived. God is fair and just. He will make it possible for you to receive these rewards if you will only trust Him and strive to live a life pleasing to Him.

And it is impossible to please God without faith. Anyone who wants to come to him must believe that God exists and that <u>he rewards those who sincerely seek him</u>. (Hebrews 11:6)

The rewards that are promised in the scripture above can most certainly be blessing and help from God during our lives on earth. For example, God can reward you with a better job, special insight to solve a difficult problem or a mate that brings great joy into your life. His rewards to us during our lives on earth can come in countless ways. However, Jesus will also grant you special recognition at His award ceremony in Heaven. And that is the focus of this chapter.

I want to make one thing very clear before we go too far in discussing God's rewards. <u>Your entrance into Heaven is not a reward</u>! A reward is something you earn based on your efforts. The Bible is clear that your salvation and eternal destination of Heaven cannot be earned. Salvation is a gift. Your salvation is based on what you believe and not on your good deeds. None of us can brag and tell God that He should let us into Heaven because we have earned it due to our exemplary life.

God saved you by his grace when you believed. And you can't take credit for this; it is a gift from God. Salvation is not a reward for the good things we have done, so none of us can boast about it. (Ephesians 2:8–9)

Jesus Christ is the only one who has never sinned. And He gave His life so that we could trust Him to provide a way to be forgiven for our sins. We would never even be eligible for the rewards ceremony unless our sins were removed first.

For God made Christ, who never sinned, to be the offering for our sin, so that we could be made right with God through Christ. (2 Corinthians 5:21)

Rewards Ceremony

Therefore we make it our aim, whether present or absent, to be well pleasing to Him. For we must all appear before <u>the judgment seat</u> of Christ, that each one may receive the things done in the body, according to what he has done, whether good or bad. (2 Corinthians 5:9–10)(NKJV)

Since we are made right with God through our faith in Jesus, this appearance before Jesus must refer to something different than a judgment for our sins. The Greek word translated "judgment seat" is the word, "bema," which means "a raised place from which judgment is rendered." For many people, the word "judgment" is usually considered to be a negative action. Maybe you received a traffic citation and went before a judge to plead your case. Unless you had a really good case, the judge probably found you guilty and charged you a fine. Or maybe you think of an extreme case in which

Chapter 7: The Judgment Seat

an individual is found guilty of murder and the judge sentences the person to death. Those are negative examples of judging.

But judging can also be a positive experience where you are rewarded for your efforts. Judges at a county fair may award you a prize for showing the best animal in your class. Reality television shows have judges who reward people for their singing or dancing ability. Olympic athletes have judges who reward the best ice skaters, ski jumpers or boxers with gold, silver or bronze medals depending on their final scores.

This "judgment seat of Christ" is a positive experience where a Christian is rewarded for the kind of life he or she chose to live. This judgment is only for those who have already been born again by trusting Jesus for their salvation. You have many opportunities to make choices in your life. The best choice you can make is to endeavor to live a life that is pleasing to God. Because every time you make a choice and take an action that is pleasing to

Him, you are creating a better rewards ceremony for yourself when you get to heaven.

Paul was a man who lived a good part of his life in opposition to God's plans and purposes. But, because of God's grace, Paul was saved from his life of rebellion and he dedicated his new life to proclaiming the good news of Jesus. The revelation Paul received about the rewards ceremony is found in the following scriptures.

Because of God's grace to me, I have laid the foundation like an expert builder. Now others are building on it. But whoever is building on this foundation must be very careful. For no one can lay any foundation other than the one we already have—Jesus Christ. (1 Corinthians 3:10–11)

Paul referenced God's grace in forgiving him of the things he did in opposition to God. Then he talked about proclaiming the foundational truth that nobody can expect to know God without understanding what Jesus did for us. Jesus is the foundation of any conversation about having a relationship with God. Without the forgiveness of our sins through Jesus, access to God is not possible. Any understanding of God has to start with Jesus.

Anyone who builds on that foundation may use a variety of materials—gold, silver, jewels, wood, hay, or straw. But on the judgment day, fire will reveal what kind of work each builder has done. The fire will show if a person's work has any value. <u>If the work survives, that builder will receive a reward</u>. (1 Corinthians 3:12–14)

After a person is saved, God begins to keep account of that individual's actions in life. Some actions have lasting value in the same way that gold, silver and jewels have lasting value. Other works are like wood, hay and straw. Those acts have little value. And when the rewards ceremony, the judgment seat of Christ, takes place, all our works will be judged to see if they are worthy of rewards. It will be as if all our works are placed in a furnace. The worthless acts of wood, hay and straw will be burned up and disappear. The significant acts that are described as gold, silver and jewels will survive the fire and remain. The works that remain will be the ones for which we are rewarded. So this ceremony can be both a joyous and a sad occasion at the same time.

But if the work is burned up, <u>the builder will suffer great loss</u>. The builder will be saved, but like someone barely escaping through a wall of flames. (1 Corinthians 3:15)

If you arrive at this place and you have nothing or very little to show for your life, you will still be saved because your trust was in Jesus for your salvation. But you will suffer a great loss of rewards you could have had if you had lived a life of obedience to God. You will come face to face with the reality of how you lived your life.

So my encouragement to you is to make a decision to live a life closer to God than ever before. Remember, God wants to forgive you of past mistakes and failures. We all have them. The only thing you can control is your future. Here are three ideas about how you can begin to accumulate rewards from God.

Stand Up For Jesus

Depending on where you live in the world, taking a public stand for Jesus can result in persecution. In some countries, a public declaration of faith in Jesus can get you killed, even beheaded. In other countries, it can result in public rejection and ridicule. Even in America, persecution of Christians is becoming more common. But I have good news for you. You will receive a great reward for publicly embracing Jesus and the truths God has revealed to us in the Bible.

What blessings await you when people hate you and exclude you and mock you and curse you as evil because you follow the Son

of Man. When that happens, be happy! Yes, leap for joy! <u>For a great reward awaits you in heaven</u>. And remember, their ancestors treated the ancient prophets that same way. (Luke 6:22–23)

Help The Needy

God has always shown mercy to those who are struggling in any area. Some struggle with a lack of money. Some have minimal education. Some are ill. Some are in bondage to an addiction of some kind. Jesus told a parable which illustrates His heart of compassion for those in need in any area. If you are willing to help someone who can never pay you back for your assistance, you are building rewards in heaven. You can help by giving money, giving your time to help or by using your talents and abilities to assist those in need.

Then he turned to his host. "When you put on a luncheon or a banquet," he said, "don't invite your friends, brothers, relatives, and rich neighbors. For they will invite you back, and that will be your only reward. Instead, invite the poor, the crippled, the lame, and the blind. Then at the resurrection of the righteous, God will reward you for inviting those who could not repay you." (Luke 14:12–14)

Run Your Race

God has plans for you and me. A critical element to living a life that is pleasing to God is to follow His plans for your life. His plans include understanding His revealed will in the Bible about decisions we make every day. And His plan involves asking for His guidance to make major life decisions such as who to marry, what career to follow or what area I should volunteer in to help in my church. We each have a race to run while we are on this earth. Finding and faithfully following God's will for that race will result in a reward one day.

As for me, my life has already been poured out as an offering to God. The time of my death is near. I have fought the good fight, <u>I have finished the race, and I have remained faithful</u>. And now the prize awaits me—the crown of righteousness, which the Lord, the righteous Judge, will give me on the day of his return. And the prize is not just for me but for all who eagerly look forward to his appearing. (2 Timothy 4:6–8)

Chapter 8
Final Judgment

"Final" can be a scary word. It is defined as, "Forming or occurring at the end." You have probably dealt with something final before. Maybe something as simple as a final exam—the last exam of that class. A popular game show has "final jeopardy"—the last trivia answer of the game. Sporting events have "the finals"—the last game, or series of games, of the season.

But "Final Judgment" carries a lot more weight than anything I have just mentioned. "Judgment" is scary enough. But the last judgment that will ever be rendered? That means everything I have done has been leading up to this event? And after this event, there is nothing I can do to change the verdict? Wow! That really is scary.

I think most people would rather not consider eternal judgment as a possibility. Especially if you understand that this final judgment will be for everything you have ever done in your life. Eternal judgment, however, is a reality. It is as certain as death. And it is one of the most basic truths revealed in the Bible.

So let us stop going over the basic teachings about Christ again and again. Let us go on instead and become mature in our understanding. Surely we don't need to start again with the fundamental importance of repenting from evil deeds and placing our faith in God. You don't need further instruction about baptisms, the laying on of hands, the resurrection of the dead, and <u>eternal judgment</u>. (Hebrews 6:1–2)

"Eternal" is another difficult word to comprehend. It means "without end, never to cease." That means that the result of this eternal judgment will go on "without end, never to cease." That also means that this world will not go on forever the way it is now. Something drastic will change when eternal judgment takes place.

One thing to remember about final, eternal judgment is that God Almighty is the final judge. He will be perfectly fair and just in His judgment. He will not be biased. He will not show any favoritism. He will judge everyone based on obedience to His will as provided to the world in His word, the Bible.

You and I are not responsible for determining a person's final spiritual destination. We do not know how to judge another person's heart or beliefs. Only God can look into a person's heart and determine its true state. Unless a person has told you what they believe, you don't really know. That is why you cannot make a final determination about another person's eternal destiny. You don't know the condition or the belief of a person's heart at the time of death. Only God knows that unless that person has shared his or her beliefs with you. So we can't judge our neighbor in the sense of sending them to heaven or hell. God's forgiveness through Jesus is available right up until a person physically dies and the spirit leaves the body.

Don't speak evil against each other, dear brothers and sisters. If you criticize and judge each other, then you are criticizing and judging God's law. But your job is to obey the law, not to judge whether it applies to you. <u>God alone, who gave the law, is the Judge</u>. He alone has the power to save or to destroy. So what right do you have to judge your neighbor? (James 4:11–12)

The standard God uses for His final judgment is perfect obedience to Him. If you have ever sinned in your life, you fall short of God's standard. And every person on earth has sinned.

For everyone has sinned; we all fall short of God's glorious standard. (Romans 3:23)

God doesn't make His final judgment based on a relative scale. You may have lived a better life than your neighbor, co-worker or sibling. You may try to reason that you haven't committed any major sins, like murder, so you should make it to heaven without a problem. But it doesn't matter whether your sin is major or minor. God doesn't compare your life with anyone else to make His final judgment. He only looks at His standard of perfection. And we all fall short of that standard.

Many people have minimalized God. They ignore the power of God that He manifested in Old Testament times. For example, God demonstrated His judgment against sin when he sent a flood to wipe out those who had become consistently evil and drifted far away from God's original plan.

"The Lord observed the extent of human wickedness on the earth, and he saw that everything they thought or imagined was consistently and totally evil. (Genesis 6:5)"

"God wiped out every living thing on the earth—people, livestock, small animals that

scurry along the ground, and the birds of the sky. All were destroyed. The only people who survived were Noah and those with him in the boat. (Genesis 7:23)"

God again demonstrated His judgment against the sexual perversion and wickedness found in the cities of Sodom and Gomorrah.

"So the Lord told Abraham, "I have heard a great outcry from Sodom and Gomorrah, because their sin is so flagrant." (Genesis 18:20)

"Then the Lord rained down fire and burning sulfur from the sky on Sodom and Gomorrah. He utterly destroyed them, along with the other cities and villages of the plain, wiping out all the people and every bit of vegetation." (Genesis 19:24–25)

Many have refused to recognize He is our Creator and He is all-powerful. Some have said He loves us all too much to send anyone to an

Chapter 8: Final Judgment

eternal punishment. That all sounds good and comforting. But it is a lie. I would be a fool and a deceiver if I did not tell you about the reality of a final judgment. God is a fair and just God. And one day the final punishment for unforgiven sin will be delivered. God doesn't want anyone to spend eternity in eternal torment. But sin is not a joke. It has consequences of a greater magnitude than many have ever imagined.

At this final judgment, millions and millions of people will be brought before Almighty God. Some will have been very famous in their lives on earth. Others will have held positions of great authority. Some will have led evil and selfish lives. Many will have led "good" lives without causing great harm to anyone. Most will be people who have led uneventful lives.

But one thing will be the same in everyone's life. Every person will be guilty of committing sin. Some more than others, but everyone will have sinned. And any amount of sin brings judgment. Final, eternal judgment and everlasting torment. Those present at this event will not have an attorney. There will be no appeals process. Only final, eternal judgment by Almighty God.

I will close this chapter with God's description of eternal judgment. He gave this vivid description to the Apostle John as He showed John many things that will happen at the end of this age. He gave John this vision for two reasons. He wanted every person to understand the reality and magnitude of this final judgment. And He also gave it as a warning because He does not want anyone to have to experience His final act concerning sin. This is a real event, and you need to know about it.

And I saw a great white throne and the one sitting on it. The earth and sky fled from his presence, but they found no place to hide. I saw the dead, both great and small, standing before God's throne. And the books were opened, including the Book of Life. And the dead were judged according to what they had done, as recorded in the books. The sea gave up its dead, and death and the grave gave up their dead. And all were judged ac-

cording to their deeds. Then death and the grave were thrown into the lake of fire. This lake of fire is the second death. <u>And anyone whose name was not found recorded in the Book of Life was thrown into the lake of fire</u>. (Revelation 20:11–15)

This will be a terrifying event. However, there is some good news I can give you about the final judgment. <u>You don't have to experience it unless you choose to</u>. If you are born again, your name will be found in the Book of Life, and you will not be present at this event. You won't be judged for your actions or thrown into the lake of fire forever because Jesus took the judgment for sin on your behalf. But your name will only be in the Book of Life if you have decided to trust Jesus for your salvation. For those not saved, this will be the most horrifying day in the history of the world. And God's decision will be final and forever.

Chapter 9
Final Thoughts

Based on all the Scriptures we have examined, judging is not something to be totally avoided. It is, however, something to be controlled. Some folks have taken the extreme position that "judge not" means they have a "get out of hell free card" and can exhibit any kind of wicked or perverse behavior without any accountability. But the other extreme is also unacceptable. Walking around with your nose in the air, pointing out everybody else's sin while ignoring your own is just as bad. So how do we bring balance to these two extremes?

"Judging" can simply mean recognizing that some behavior is harmful. Sin is harmful conduct. It may seem enjoyable for a while, but it will eventually have a bad result. The reason

God warns us against sin is because He does not want us to be hurt. He also recognizes that continual sin will lead a person further and further away from God. Developing a relationship with God requires time. It takes time to read the Bible to understand God's character and nature and His wisdom for our lives. It takes time to pray consistently to talk to God about our needs and to listen to Him as He communicates with us by His Spirit. Spending time with God causes us to grow up and mature as a Christian. Once you are born again, you have to take action to grow up or you will remain a baby Christian. The more mature you are, the easier it is to recognize the difference between "right and wrong."

You have been believers so long now that you ought to be teaching others. Instead, you need someone to teach you again the basic things about God's word. You are like babies who need milk and cannot eat solid food. For someone who lives on milk is still an infant and doesn't know how to do what *is right. Solid food is for <u>those who are mature</u>, who through training have the skill to <u>recognize the difference between right and wrong</u>. (Hebrews 5:12–14)*

Rest assured, there will be a day when Jesus will return to earth and judge everyone according to His truth and His revelation of what is right and wrong. That's why it is so important to preach, or proclaim, the truth found in God's word. Even when people oppose you and ridicule you and it doesn't look like it's a good time to share the truth with your fellow believers, speak it anyway. Maturing as a Christian means learning to have the wisdom to "...*speak the truth in love...(Ephesians 4:15)*." We always need to be humble and gentle in the way we communicate, but also realize that the truth is the standard by which we will be judged.

I solemnly urge you in the presence of God and Christ Jesus, who will someday judge the living and the dead when he comes to set up his Kingdom: Preach the word of God. Be prepared, whether the time is favorable or not. Patiently correct, rebuke, and encourage your people with good teaching. (2 Timothy 4:1-2)

The Bible says to "patiently" correct, rebuke and encourage with God's word. Being patient means to remember that maturing takes time. Nobody grows up quickly. We learn and mature and growth is a process. When you have an opportunity to speak to a believer about his conduct, don't demand perfection and immediate change. Give him time to process and absorb what you have said. If you present your concerns with the right attitude, your input will probably be considered.

Notice the three things Paul said to do when we proclaim the truth of God's word.

1. Correct—This is really a rather harsh word. The full meaning includes rebuke, admonish, to call to account, to show one his fault and to chasten. Most people

don't want to do any of those things. But, when you share the word of God without apology, it can sting when it points out our faults.
2. Rebuke—This word means to clearly warn a person of the consequences of his actions.
3. Encourage—This word means to provide positive support that a person can recover from sinful mistakes and make better choices in the future. Everyone needs to know that there is hope for a better tomorrow.

There will always be people who choose to reject God and rebel against any kind of correction. Some folks will only listen to people who tell them their behavior is just fine and that nobody has the right to tell them anything different. Some have even bought into the myth that there are no consequences for their actions because God will overlook and forgive everybody's sin and allow everybody into heaven. The Bible warns us about people like that.

For a time is coming when people will no longer listen to sound and wholesome teaching. They will follow their own desires and will look for teachers who will tell them whatever their itching ears want to hear. They will reject the truth and chase after myths. (2 Timothy 4:3–4)

So what about Jesus' words about judging? **"Judge not, that you be not judged. (Matthew 7:1)(NKJV).** How can we balance what He said with everything else we have looked at in this book? In order to properly interpret Scripture, we need to know the context of the passage we are studying. The Bible was not written in chapters and verses. Those were added later to aid in organization and understanding. When we look back into the 6th chapter of Matthew, we find that Jesus is rebuking the religious leaders of the day for their hypocritical behavior. A "hypocrite" is an actor. An actor pretends to be someone he is not when he takes on a role.

For example, Jesus rebuked folks for their hypocrisy in making a big show of giving money to the poor. They were doing it to be recognized for their goodness instead of a genuine desire to help the needy. He rebuked those who made a big show of praying publicly to gain notoriety for being so pious. Jesus told them to pray to the Father in private if they were serious. And Jesus rebuked those who made a show of fasting by making sure everyone knew the sacrifice they were making. Jesus told them to keep it private so only God knew what they were doing.

The 7th chapter of Matthew is a continuation of Jesus' teaching on avoiding hypocrisy. We know that believers should not be judging unbelievers. And we know that we need to have the proper, humble, gentle attitude to judge fellow believers. Jesus primarily dealt with hypocritical judging of others in this portion of His discourse.

"Do not judge others, and you will not be judged. For you will be treated as you treat others. The standard you use in judging is the standard by which you will be judged.

"And why worry about a speck in your friend's eye when you have a log in your own? How can you think of saying to your friend, 'Let me help you get rid of that speck in your eye,' when you can't see past the log in your own eye? Hypocrite! First get rid of the log in your own eye; then you will see well enough to deal with the speck in your friend's eye. (Matthew 7:1–5)

Jesus had harsh words for hypocrites on several occasions. Jesus used hyperbole to illustrate His point in the passage above. He said to deal with the major or frequent sins in your own life before you start pointing out the sin in your friend's life. His exaggerated example was that the plank, or log, in your own eye is far greater than the speck you want to point out in your friend's eye. Jesus' point was that you should deal with your own problems before you go on a fault-finding mission of your friend's behavior.

Also note that Jesus said after you deal with your sin (the log), you will be better able to focus on your friend's needs (the speck). So judging, or recognizing sin, in someone else's life is certainly permissible. However, you should make sure you have repented and been forgiven of your own sins before you help someone else deal with their sin. Hypocritical judging is unacceptable behavior in God's eyes. This is especially true if you are guilty of committing the same sins you are condemning in someone else.

You may think you can condemn such people, but you are just as bad, and you have no excuse! When you say they are wicked and should be punished, you are condemning yourself, for you who judge others do these very same things. And we know that God, in his justice, will punish anyone who does such things. Since you judge others for doing these things, why do you think you can avoid God's judgment when you do the same things? (Romans 2:1–3)

Finally, remember that we all need God's grace and mercy. We all deal with various sins in our lives. None of us can boast of never giving in to temptation. So humility is critical before you consider approaching people about their sinful behavior. However, a good friend will want to help a friend escape from the bondage of sin. And with the right attitude and a humble heart, we can strengthen each other in our own time of need.

Dear brothers and sisters, if another believer is overcome by some sin, you who are godly should gently and humbly help that person back onto the right path. And be careful not to fall into the same temptation yourself. Share each other's burdens, and in this way obey the law of Christ. (Galatians 6:1–2)

The Big Picture

1. Consider everything the Bible says about judging before making a judgment about judging.

Chapter 9: Final Thoughts

2. God's word, the Bible, is the standard for all judgment.
3. Judging conduct as right or wrong is a sign of maturity and not a sign of hate.
4. Judging and dealing with your own sin is the most important aspect of judging.
5. Believers judging believers is part of life, but only with the right attitude.
6. Judging unbelievers is God's business alone.
7. Believers will be rewarded for living good lives.
8. Final judgment for sin is inevitable and forever.
9. Hypocritical judging is never acceptable.

About the Author

RANDY CLARK HAS BEEN TEACHING THE TRUTHS OF the Bible since graduating from Victory Bible Institute in Tulsa, Oklahoma in 1980.

He has served as a Pastor, Bible School Instructor, Church Planter and Christian Television Station Manager. His ministry has also included a weekly television program and a daily radio outreach.

Randy's ministry travels have taken him across the United States and into foreign countries as close as Canada and Mexico and as far away as Indonesia and Ukraine.

He is the author of numerous books and magazine articles and is the founder of Randy Clark Ministries, a world-wide teaching and training ministry. For more resources from the author visit his website at:

www.RandyClark.info

If this book was a help to you, please go to the Amazon.com listing for the book and leave a review. This will encourage others to take advantage of the information and inspiration found within these pages. This book is also available in Kindle and Audible formats through Amazon.com.

www.ingramcontent.com/pod-product-compliance
Lightning Source LLC
Chambersburg PA
CBHW060339080526
44584CB00013B/844